MARY NOHL

Other Badger Biographies

MARY NOHL

A LIFETIME IN ART

BARBARA MANGER
AND JANINE SMITH

WISCONSIN HISTORICAL SOCIETY PRESS

Published by the Wisconsin Historical Society Press
Publishers since 1855

©2013 by State Historical Society of Wisconsin

For permission to reuse material from *Mary Nohl: A Lifetime in Art* (978-0-87020-577-4), please access www.copyright.com or contact the Copyright Clearance Center, Inc. (CCC), 222 Rosewood Drive, Danvers, MA 01923, 978-750-8400. CCC is a not-for-profit organization that provides licenses and registration for a variety of users.

wisconsin**history**.org

A list of illustration credits can be found on pages 120–123, which constitute a continuation of this copyright page.

Printed in Wisconsin, U.S.A.
Designed by Jill Bremigan

17 16 15 14 13   1 2 3 4 5

Library of Congress Cataloging-in-Publication Data

Manger, Barbara, 1943-
    Mary Nohl : a lifetime in art / Barbara Manger and Janine Smith. — 1 [edition].
       pages cm — (Badger biographies series)
    Includes index.
    ISBN 978-0-87020-577-4 (pbk. : alk. paper) 1. Nohl, Mary, 1914-2001—Juvenile literature.
2. Artists—United States—Biography—Juvenile literature. 3. Artists—Wisconsin—Biography—
Juvenile literature. I. Title.
    N6537.N648M36 2013
    709.2—dc23
    [B]
                            2012032703

Front cover: Photograph courtesy of Ron Byers
Front cover background: Shapes derived from Mary's front gate, circa 1963, and fence, circa 1973, at Mary Nohl's Lake Cottage Environment. Courtesy of the John Michael Kohler Arts Center Artist Archives
Back cover: Mary Nohl, *Self-portraits,* ca. 1933-1936. Courtesy of the John Michael Kohler Arts Center Artist Archives

∞ The paper used in this publication meets the minimum requirements of the American National Standard for Information Sciences—Permanence of Paper for Printed Library Materials, ANSI Z39.48-1992.

For our grandchildren
Max and Will
Molly, Kasey, and Lucy

Publication of this book was made possible in part by a
gift from the Kohler Foundation.

Contents

1

The Witch's House

In the Milwaukee **suburb** of Fox Point, Beach Drive is a fine place for a walk. On the east side of the road is beautiful Lake Michigan. The lake is so big you cannot see the other side. The sandy beach is touched by waves and dotted with smooth stones and **driftwood**. On the west side of the road, the houses have big windows and the lawns and gardens are well kept. If you keep walking, you will come upon a strange and wonderful sight.

One of the statues outside "the witch's house"

suburb: homes and shopping centers beyond the main settled areas of a city   driftwood: wood that has spent a long time floating in a lake or ocean and is sometimes washed up on shore

1

At a curve in the road a big wire fence encloses a yard and house unlike any you have ever seen. If you peek through the fence, you will see huge heads made of **concrete**. You will see life-size **figures** of people, fish, and other creatures. If you look again you will see that this house is different from all the other houses on the road.

If the gate is unlocked, you can enter and tiptoe even closer. You will see small black stones that spell out the word "BOO" on the doorstep. If you look up, you will see wooden cutouts of people hanging from the tree branches and swaying in the breeze. You will hear the swish of waves washing up on the beach.

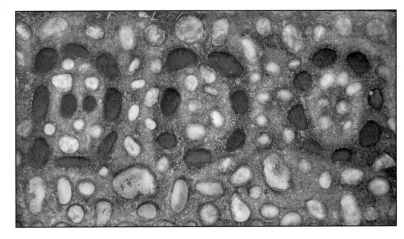

This is what you'll see if you get to the front porch. Does it scare you?

concrete: a building material made up of sand, gravel, cement, and water that becomes very hard when it dries
figure: a shape or outline

2

If you are curious, you might ask a neighbor walking past, "Who lives here?" The neighbor might answer, "Nobody now, but a woman who was called a witch once lived here. She made all of this. She worked every day for many years building one thing, then another. Sometimes she was in the yard or up on a ladder, sometimes she was on the roof, but she was always working."

You might ask, "Who was this **mysterious** person?" You might wonder, "How did she make all of this?" and "Why?"

The answer to these questions starts with a name: Mary Nohl. Mary was an artist who lived and worked in the house on the lakeshore for many years. Mary's sculptures filled the yard. Art made of every material imaginable filled the house.

Mary lived her entire life doing the thing she loved most: making art.

mysterious (mi **stir** ee uhs): hard to understand or explain

3

2

Childhood Adventures

This is the true story of Mary Louise Nohl, who was not a witch at all. She was a real child like most other children. She was born in 1914 in the city of Milwaukee, Wisconsin. Her father, **Leo** Nohl, was a successful lawyer. Her mother, Emma, was a talented singer. They both were of German **descent**. Mary had one brother, **Eugene Maximilian**, called Max, who was 4 years older.

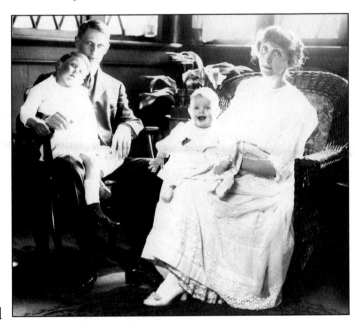

The Nohl family in 1914. Baby Mary is happy on her mother's lap. Max sits on Leo's lap.

Leo: lee oh   **descent** (di **sent**): from a certain country or culture   **Eugene Maximilian**: **yoo** jeen mak suh **mil** yuhn

Emma and Leo Nohl loved their children, but they were very **strict**. They believed that children should be seen and not heard. This was often difficult for Max and Mary. Max was serious, but Mary was happy and carefree. She was also playful and full of energy, but always tried to behave nicely around adults.

Mary said, "My parents were never afraid to take me anywhere. When asked how I was, I would grin and say 'fine.' ... I never said the wrong thing because I never said anything more than just 'fine.'"

The Nohl family lived in this house on Stowell Avenue in Milwaukee when Mary was young. Mary and her friends liked to play under the porch.

strict: making sure all the rules are followed

The Nohl family lived in a big house on the east side of Milwaukee. Mary and her neighborhood friends— Wally, Georgia, Helen, Sonny, Charlotte, and Jane—created their own fun. Television and video games had not been invented. The neighborhood was their playground and Mary, the leader, was full of creative ideas for games and activities.

Mary and her gang built puppet theaters and put on shows for the younger children. They made dolls and **hobbyhorses** out of wood scraps. They spent many hours exploring. They climbed trees for good views of what was

SKETCHED AND FULLY COMPLETED BY MARY LOUISE NOHL, AGE FIVE IIIII IIII IIII IIII IIII

Mary's mother saved everything, even this pencil drawing Mary made when she was 5.

hobbyhorse: a child's toy made of a stick with a fake horse's head on one end

6

happening in the neighborhood. To travel from one yard to another they jumped over bushes and fences. This was more fun than using the sidewalks. They raced their bikes up and down the streets. With an old wooden box, a steel handle, and some wheels they built a pretend **trolley car**. They charged other children a penny to hop on board and clunk along the sidewalk.

Mary liked going fast. While roller-skating, she held on as her big dog Jack pulled her along on his leash. For more thrills, she tried to fly by jumping off the porch railing holding an umbrella. She tried this many times but she never flew.

The children were happy to discover that they could crawl underneath the Nohls' front porch. It was a perfect spot to hold secret meetings of the "under the porch club." To brighten the dark space they decorated the porch walls with crayons. Hidden from the eyes of adults, they also made treasure maps and wrote secret notes. They sealed the maps in old bottles with melted crayon wax to keep them safe from

trolley car: a type of car that runs on tracks on a city street and is powered by electricity

intruders. They planned surprise attacks on their enemies. Their weapons were hand-carved swords. Their shields were garbage can lids. The battles were pretend only, and nobody got hurt.

In winter, Mary and her friends made little snow houses and curled up inside them until they were freezing cold. After the holidays, they piled together Christmas trees to make forts. In a nearby field, they dug a hole and laid boards across the top for a roof to make an underground hideout. Mary and her pal Wally also built a little house from a wooden piano box and lumber scraps. On the walls inside they

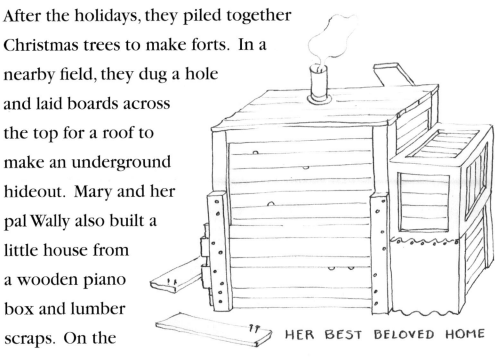

HER BEST BELOVED HOME

Mary drew "her best beloved home" when she was an adult, remembering what fun it was.

intruder: a person who goes into a place without permission

8

pasted comic strips from the newspaper for wallpaper. Mary and Wally spent many happy hours playing in their cozy little house. She called it "her best beloved home."

Gathering bits and pieces of junk was one of Mary's favorite hobbies. She collected just about anything, even the colorful gold and red paper **cigar bands** tossed away by men who smoked cigars. Then she pasted them together to make a bright **design**. All through her life, she collected the things other people threw away. When Mary became an artist, she would use junk and other **found objects** to make her art. She liked the idea of using old things in new ways.

Mary also liked using the tools from her father Leo's workbench. Leo encouraged Mary's interest in building as long as she kept his tools in perfect order. In 1927, she began eighth grade in Hartford Avenue School. Her father talked the principal into letting Mary join the boys' **shop class**. Girls usually studied sewing and cooking in **home economics class**. But Leo knew that she would prefer shop class.

---

cigar band: a loop of paper or foil wrapped on a cigar that shows its brand   **design**: di ᴢɪɴ
found object: something that wasn't made to be art but that an artist takes and uses in a new artistic way
shop class: class where skills like carpentry are taught   **home economics class**: class where skills like sewing and cooking are taught

BEATS BOYS, 'TIS PLANE

As a model airplane builder, Mary, who is only 13, proved superior to a group of boys. Her plane placed first twice in competition with twenty-six planes built by boys in a contest at the Hartford Avenue Social center last night. She lives at 773 Stowell av.

—By a Wisconsin News Staff Photographer.

MARY NOHL

A plane, built by a girl, defeated those made by the boys in two classes in the model plane contest at the Hartford Avenue Social center last night. Mary Nohl, 13, 773 Stowell av., competing against twenty-six planes built by boys, won the junior commercial and junior weight carrying contests.

Last night marked the close of the district contests. The finals will be held March 31 or April 7, probably in the Public Service building auditorium. The contests have been held under the supervision of the school board extension department with R. C. Miller in charge. The air service committee of the Milwaukee Association of Commerce, which has been sponsoring the contests, has arranged for $500 in prizes in addition to airplane rides over the city.

A paper clip and rubber band helped Mary's plane fly for 13 seconds to win the contest.

Shop class was perfect for Mary. She learned to use every tool. In a class contest, Mary sanded a block of wood smoother than any other student's block. The prize was a small carving knife, which she treasured and used her whole life.

In March 1928, Mary was the only girl to enter the school's model-plane flying contest. She built a plane from **balsa** wood and paper. To everyone's surprise, her plane flew longer than any of the boys' planes. She won first place! The prize was $500 and a ride on a small airplane. That April, she entered the **citywide** contest.

balsa (bawl suh): a really light wood that comes from a tropical tree   **citywide**: involving a whole city

Minutes before Mary's turn, a newspaper photographer picked up her plane. He wanted to look more closely at the little paper clip and rubber band **device** that Mary had made to **propel** the plane. By accident, he broke her delicate plane. Mary was sad that she could not take part in the contest. The photographer was sad too and he apologized. Later, Mary repaired her model plane and kept it for her whole life. When she was 80 years old, she hung the plane so that it twirled from her bedroom ceiling. It reminded her of the time she began building and creating. Mary **graduated** from Hartford Avenue School in 1928 with good grades, earning G's (good) in shop class and E's (excellent) in drawing.

In 1924, the Nohl family bought land "out in the country" on Beach Drive on the shore of Lake Michigan. The land was a 45-minute drive from their house in Milwaukee. They enjoyed picnics, bonfires, and beach walks. They saw deer and foxes. Mary and her father built 2 stone and concrete posts to mark the entrance to their property. This is the place where Mary would make her mark in the world.

device: a piece of equipment that does a particular job   **propel**: move something forward
graduated (**graj** oo ay tud): finished school

Fox Point

Lake House
7238 North
Beach Drive

WISCONSIN

MILWAUKEE

Lake Michigan

City House
3017 North
Stowell Ave.

East Milwaukee

MILWAUKEE

The family built a small cottage on the property and spent their summers there. Mary liked being close to the lake. There were only a few houses along the beach at the time. Her friend Johnny **Willetts** lived in one of them. He and Mary began a lifelong friendship. They played on the sand and in the woods. They built little boats to race in the creek that flowed into the lake. On warm days, they swam in Lake Michigan and made rafts from logs that washed up on the beach. When Johnny was an old man, he remembered the fun he had playing by the lake with Mary. He remembered that Mary liked to **perch** on a rock that stuck out of the water. She sat there to watch the changing moods of the lake and sky. Everyone in the neighborhood called it "Mary's rock."

Mary **put down her roots** here. She loved her home on Lake Michigan and felt connected to it. The beach and the lake, the sunsets and the trees were part of her world. Here, with stones, wood, cement, and paint she would create a **unique** space that would become part of the natural **environment**.

Willetts: **wil** uhts   perch: sit or stand on the edge of something   **put down her roots**: made someplace her home and became connected to it   **unique** (yoo **neek**): the only one of its kind
environment (en **vi** ruhn muhnt): a place and its surroundings

13

Keeping a Diary

When Mary was 12 years old she began to write about her life in a diary. One of her first **entries** was about a hike from Milwaukee to Fox Point. She wrote, "Got pussy willows. . . . Got a couple of . . . worms in the face. . . . Saw a robin. . . . Played 'keep away' and got all full of mud." When she began high school, the diary became Mary's silent friend. She wrote exactly 8 lines every single day. Her handwriting was so tiny that she managed to fit many words on every line. She also squeezed many memories into each little diary. Keeping a record of her life was important to Mary.

Sometimes she wrote about ordinary events. "Bought thirty-six **pints** of toffee ice cream on special at Walgreens," one entry read. Her dogs and other pets—including 2 monkeys and baby raccoons that she kept in her childhood playhouse—

Many years of memories fill Mary's diaries. You need a magnifying glass to read her tiny writing!

entry: a piece of information in a book such as a diary or dictionary   **pint** (pint): a small container

14

were a favorite topic. She also recorded arguments with friends or with her brother, Max. When she was an adult, she wrote about building the big concrete heads in her yard and about her plans for other sculptures. Sometimes she wrote about the news of the day. On October 2, 1933, Mary wrote that she had seen President Franklin D. Roosevelt driving past the Art Institute of Chicago. That day, he had been in Chicago to deliver a speech.

"There is some kind of **drive** that keeps me writing in them," she said. Every day until September 13, 1995, Mary wrote her 8 lines. When she was 81 and her health began to fail, she stopped writing. In her old age, she enjoyed remembering her life by reading her diaries.

drive: a longing or need to do something

3
Learning to Be an Artist

At age 14, Mary was 5 feet 9 inches tall with hair as straight as a stick and big feet. Perhaps she felt **awkward** and **self-conscious** when she entered Milwaukee University School, a private high school near her home. Luckily years of swimming, camping, and hard work around her family's Fox Point property had made her strong. She loved sports and was excited to join the swimming, volleyball, and basketball teams.

School was challenging and Mary studied hard. "I had my father buy me some eyeglasses because I thought they would make me think harder," Mary wrote in her diary.

It is no surprise that Mary's favorite high school class was **mechanical drawing**. She loved the art supplies: pencils, paints, and **compasses**. She was good at drawing and spent

awkward: clumsy   self-conscious (self **kon** shuhs): worried about how you look to other people
mechanical drawing: a drawing made with rulers and compasses   **compass**: a tool with 2 legs and a movable joint, used for drawing circles and arcs

many hours in the art room. She had plenty of friends and a busy **social life**.

In June of 1932 she graduated from Milwaukee University School. She was longing for adventure and freedom, so when it was time to go to college Mary went as far away as possible. She chose Rollins College in Winter Park, Florida, more than 1,000 miles from Milwaukee.

Mary was busy with many activities in high school. She especially liked playing sports.

Life was very different in the 1930s than it is today. The stock market had crashed in 1928. Many people were out of work. They called it the **Great Depression**. Families did everything they could to keep their homes. Some children had to work to help their families. Every single penny was saved for rent and food. It was a daily struggle. Mary was

social life: the time you spend having fun with friends   **Great Depression**: the decade of the 1930s when many people in the United States had no job and were very poor

very lucky. Her family could afford to send her to college. Even so, they didn't waste money. Mary learned in college how to save her money and to use and **reuse** the things she owned. If she was careful, a pair of **stockings** could last Mary a whole month.

Outdoor painting was Mary's favorite class at Rollins College, 1933.

During college, Mary discovered that she loved finding treasures in the local dump. She collected some amazing stuff. While she was away at college, she wrote letters home twice a week. It was the best way to communicate with her parents and receive information from home. In a letter to her father she wrote, "I wish you could see my room ... red, green, blue, and yellow streamers on the

reuse: use again   **stocking**: a pair of thin, delicate tights that are easily torn

18

ceiling across strings with a background of palm branches.
Jump ropes, valentines, cotton chickens, paper snowballs,
Mickey Mouse, rubber peanuts, pipe cleaner animals, wooden
and wire dogs . . . hang **suspended** from the . . . strings."

Imagine that room! Her parents would never have
allowed it at home!

Mary loved her art classes. She took her first sculpture
class at Rollins. In that class, Mary learned to work with clay
and how to construct **plaster molds**. (Later in her life, Mary
used plaster molds in her **pottery** shop). "Drawing from

At Rollins, Mary learned the steps to making pottery, which requires digging, mixing,
and pouring clay into a plaster mold as shown here in her **sketch**.

suspended: attached to something and hanging downward   **plaster mold**: a container in a particular shape,
which makes anything poured into it, when dried, into that shape   **pottery**: containers made of wet clay that
is then hardened in a hot oven   **sketch**: a simple drawing

Nature" was her favorite. The students painted outside. Mary loved painting the clouds. They reminded her of her life on Lake Michigan.

Travel Journals

Emma and Leo introduced Mary to the pleasure of travel, something Mary enjoyed throughout her life. In 1927, when she was 14, Mary traveled with her parents and her brother Max on a cruise ship to Cuba, **Haiti**, and **Jamaica**. The trip was long. They first traveled to Chicago. Mary was so excited that she put her dress on inside out! Then they took a train to Miami, Florida, where they boarded a ship. Sailing on the Atlantic Ocean on a big ship was a thrilling new experience. The ship sailed to many places, including **Havana**, Cuba, where they went ashore. Mary was a **keen** observer and wanted to remember everything she saw. In a tiny blue notebook titled "My Trip" she wrote about poor children begging on the streets of Havana and about seeing tall palm trees for the first time.

Mary created a special book for each of her trips.

Haiti: hay tee   **Jamaica:** juh **may** kuh   **Havana:** huh **van** uh   **keen:** eager, enthusiastic

Curious and **adventuresome**, Mary traveled to many countries and **exotic** places during her lifetime. For each trip, she put together a travel journal using paper, cardboard, fabric, needle, and thread. The books were a good way to save postcards, menus, coins, stamps, and photographs.

There were lots of social activities at Rollins, including tea parties, dances, bonfires, picnics, and going on dates. It was a fun time and Mary felt comfortable at college. Her confidence led to adventures. She was far more daring than her classmates. Mary **hitchhiked** around Florida with a friend. At that time women did not travel alone and hitchhiking was forbidden by the school. On another one of her adventures she ended up spending the night in an old run-down shack.

She loved playing **pranks** on her friends. She would **short-sheet** their beds, hide her roommate's clothes, and put **petroleum jelly** on the doorknob to prevent the door from opening. Some of these pranks got her into trouble. Not everyone understood Mary's sense of humor. She was never

adventuresome: willing to go on an adventure **exotic**: strange and interesting **hitchhiked**: got rides in strangers' cars by standing on the side of the road and waiting for someone to stop **prank**: a playful trick **short-sheet**: to fold and tuck the sheets on someone's bed so that the person can't get all the way in **petroleum** (puh **troh** lee uhm) **jelly**: an oily substance often used in medicines and makeup

afraid to say what she thought and sometimes this led to problems with her friendships.

Mary was having fun, but her parents were concerned that she was not learning enough at Rollins. Her father had a big **influence** over Mary and felt that there was more to school than her social life. So, Mary left Rollins. In September of 1933 Mary enrolled at the Art **Institute** of Chicago, one of the best art schools in the world.

The work at the Art Institute was much more challenging than at Rollins. Her letters home were full of what she was learning: "[I am] studying muscles in the body, working on the alphabet in **lettering** class and on **color charts** in design class."

Mary spent 6 years at the Art Institute. Her days were filled with a variety of art classes. In her drawing and painting classes she painted the human figure. She also painted **still-life compositions** of objects like food, flowers, and books. Mary was excited to try the different kinds of paints like

influence: the ability to get someone to think or behave in a certain way   **institute** (**in** stuh toot): a building or organization with a specific goal   **lettering**: the art of drawing and writing the letters of the alphabet in special ways, such as for a sign or a greeting card   **color chart**: a piece of paper with squares of different colors on it, used to check colors and make sure they are correct and go well together   **still-life composition**: a painting or drawing of objects that aren't moving

oil paint, **watercolor**, and **egg tempera**. Mary loved to learn and the Art Institute of Chicago gave her the opportunity to explore.

Mary was a quick learner and her **self-confidence** grew. The Art Institute was buzzing with creative ideas and people. Artists came from all over the United States and the world to **lecture** on art. Mary wrote home about a chubby little artist from Cedar Rapids, Iowa, who gave lectures. Grant Wood became famous for his paintings, especially *American Gothic.*

At the Art Institute, Mary began to **mature**

Mary admired the work of Grant Wood. He was very famous for this painting, *American Gothic.*

oil paint: a type of paint that uses oil mixed with color   watercolor: a type of paint that uses water mixed with color   egg tempera: a type of paint that uses the white part of an egg mixed with color   self-confidence: belief in one's abilities and worth   lecture: give a talk to an audience, often at a college or university   mature (muh **chur**): become more grown up as an artist. She carried a drawing pad with her at all times and drew constantly. Like a sponge, Mary soaked up everything. She was learning to love art—all the time. She worked 12 hours a day on her artwork. There was so much to learn. Nothing escaped Mary's interest, from poetry to psychology.

She visited the Field Museum in Chicago. There she discovered art from Africa, Australia, and **Easter Island**. She went to the theater, opera, films, and political events. Her girlfriends had poetry readings and discussions on friendship. She was living the life of an artist.

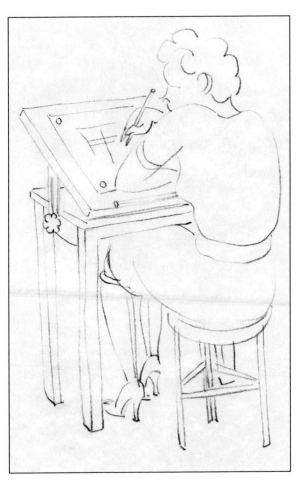

Mary drew herself in every possible position.

Easter Island: an island in the Pacific Ocean

In the summer of 1935, she and 2 friends toured Europe. They sailed across the Atlantic Ocean and visited France, Germany, Belgium, Italy, Switzerland, England, Portugal, and **Algiers**. They took in all the sights and scenery, old castles, museums, and famous **cathedrals**. It was a magnificent trip.

Mary never tired of drawing herself. She always worked to improve her skill.

Mary's friends were very curious and excited about art and culture just like she was. At the Art Institute, she felt at home among all the art students. Ideas and knowledge were more important than how she dressed or how many friends she had.

Algiers: al **jirz**   **cathedral** (kuh **thee** druhl): a large church

25

Mary's favorite teacher was her **figure-drawing** instructor, Edmund **Giesbert**. She took notes in his classes and went over and over them after class was over. He encouraged her to draw everything in sight, and she did! She drew her classmates, her room, views from her window, and even herself. Mr. Giesbert's lectures inspired her. He taught her to have courage, to "make up your mind and do something." Her desire to learn was endless and her ability in drawing grew under his teaching.

figure drawing: drawing of the human body   **Giesbert: geez** bert

4

Danny Diver

While Mary was learning to be an artist, her older brother, Max, was exploring the underwater world.

When Max was a boy he was fascinated with the stories of the many shipwrecks in Lake Michigan. His dad told him about the huge storms that rocked the great ships until they **capsized**. He dreamed of the captains on these big **cargo ships** that sank and of the treasures that lay on the bottom of the lake floor.

In 1920, Max was 10 and Mary was 6.

capsized: tipped over   **cargo ship**: a ship that carries goods like salt, wheat, or lumber

27

Max and his friends built log rafts with cloth sails. They had sailing adventures on Lake Michigan and pretended to be pirates. Like Mary, Max was influenced by his life on the shores of Lake Michigan.

Max was 4 years older than Mary. Imagine the 2 of them playing creative games on their lake property. The truth is that Mary and Max did not always get along. When Mary was 12, Max went into her room and found her secret box. It was locked but Max forced it open. He read her personal letters and looked through her diaries. She was furious! The next week she got even. She went into his room and discovered *his* secret box and read through his stuff. After that they stopped speaking to each other for a long time.

Mary was glad when Max went off to college at the **Massachusetts** Institute of **Technology**. There he continued to be interested in the underwater world. At school he worked on developing a **capsule** that was big enough to carry one person deep down into the sea. It looked like a miniature, round submarine. Max called it a "diving bell." During the

Massachusetts: mas uh **choo** sits　**technology** (tek **nol** uh jee): the use of science to do practical things
capsule (**kap** suhl): a container

summer he brought the bell home and tried it out in Lake Michigan. The next year he took it to the **Caribbean** where he experimented in the ocean waters.

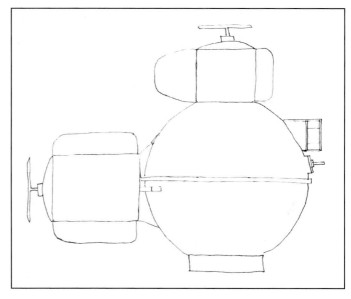

Max drew this picture of his diving bell design. A small window helped the person inside see where he or she was going. The motor moved the diving bell around underwater.

He knew if he wanted to explore the deep waters he needed 2 things. He needed to be able to breathe underwater and he needed to protect his skin from the cold. With the help of Dr. Edgar End from **Marquette** College in Milwaukee, he learned how to mix the right combination of oxygen and helium. This allowed him stay underwater longer. Then he experimented with making a diving suit. It had to be easy to put on, waterproof, and not too heavy. This was a time when

Caribbean (cair ruh **bee** uhn or cair **ri** bee uhn): the sea between North and South America
Marquette: mahr **ket**

the underwater world was virtually unexplored. Lots of people were interested in what Max was doing. He was a **fascinating** character.

One icy day in December 1937, Max tested the diving suit in Lake Michigan. It worked! Max was lowered 420 feet. That was the deepest dive anyone had made. He became world famous! No one had ever done what Max did. Now he could explore all the sunken ships in Lake Michigan and beyond.

Max is lowered into the freezing cold water of Lake Michigan. It took 2 tries before he made it to the bottom.

fascinating: very interesting

30

Max became an expert on deep-sea **exploration** and sunken ships. After the dive, he went around the world talking to audiences about his experience. He also tried many times to find sunken treasures, but he never succeeded at finding anything valuable.

During this time everyone was interested in Max and his underwater explorations. As the little sister, no one paid much attention to Mary. Even though Mary felt left out, she talked to Max about his discoveries.

Max told Mary about all the interesting things he saw on the ocean floor. He experimented with an underwater movie camera that could film the underwater world, and he showed the pictures to Mary. She was fascinated. This was the first time Mary had seen what lies far below the ocean's waves. While Mary was still in art school, she and Max **collaborated** on ideas for a book. Mary began writing and illustrating a children's cartoon book called *Danny Diver.*

It took Mary about 5 years to finish the story about Danny, a lonely deep-sea diver who goes to the bottom of the sea

exploration: studying or discovering an unknown thing   **collaborated**: worked together

31

Danny Diver looked for friends
at the bottom of the ocean.

India ink: a special type of dark black ink

looking for friends. He has lots
of adventures with mermaids and
big happy fish and seahorses and
underground cities. Something
exciting always happens to Danny,
but he rarely finds what he is
looking for—friends.

The pencil and ink drawings
in the book are imaginative
and cheerful. Mary made many
sketches as she planned the
book. She made the sketches with
India ink and watercolors. She
experimented with the size of the
images and the way they would
look in the book. In many ways the
story mirrored the lives of Max and
Mary. Sometimes they succeeded,
and sometimes they had to try

A set of cartoons from *Danny Diver*

again. For years Mary tried to get the book published, but it never happened.

Max and Mary's friendship went up and down during their adult years. When Max died many years later in a car accident, Mary was shocked. It was a "new **sensation** to be an only child," she wrote in her diary.

sensation: feeling

5

The Art of Teaching

After finishing her studies at the Art Institute, Mary realized that it would be difficult to make a living by being an artist.

Mary's watercolor of an art teacher at work

She thought that teaching art would be the next best thing. So, she spent an extra year at the Art Institute studying art education. Eventually, she found a job in Maryland.

She was a traveling art teacher for 4 different schools. At noon she would pack up her supplies and head to a different school.

Teaching was hard work but she was lucky to have a job. The year 1940 marked the beginning of World War II. Many of Mary's friends and neighbors were fighting in the war. It was a lonely time for Mary living in a small town far away from the Midwest. After 2 years of teaching in Maryland, she came home to Milwaukee.

Mary was glad to return to Milwaukee and her Midwest roots. She moved back home into her old familiar room. She looked up her old girlfriends and jumped right into a busy social life. She went bowling and ice skating, went to the movies and to dinner parties, and even took dance lessons. Many of her friends were getting married and having babies. Mary was a little jealous. She dated a few men but never developed that special relationship she was longing for. She knew she wanted a productive life, so after a few months of being home, she started searching for a job.

She found a job teaching art at North Division High School. After one semester, she switched to **Steuben** Middle School. There, she met Rosalind "**Ros**" **Couture**, another art teacher. Ros taught sixth and seventh grade and Mary taught eighth grade. Their classrooms were next door to each other. Mary and Ros became lifelong friends. Their teaching styles were very different. Ros's classroom was noisy and chaotic. Kids were running around laughing and art supplies were everywhere. In contrast, Mary played classical music and all the students sat at their desks. Mary was a strict disciplinarian and wanted quiet and order.

Mary, right, poses with her best friend, Ros.

Mary talked her principal into buying a **kiln**, and began teaching a **ceramics** class. For a while this kept Mary's interest, but soon she started dreaming of having her own kiln and pottery shop. She

Steuben: stoi ben   **Ros Couture: roz** koo **tur**   **kiln**: a very hot oven used to bake and harden clay
ceramics (ser **a** miks): pottery

came home at night and mixed clay in the bathtub. She said, "My bathroom is the clay works now." Can you imagine what her mom and dad thought? That next year Ros left Milwaukee and moved to Massachusetts. Mary was unhappy. She didn't quit teaching but she made a plan.

That summer she worked as an **apprentice** at South Milwaukee Pottery Company and studied all the basic steps in pottery making. In the fall she went back to teaching, but her heart wasn't in it. Mary said, "The kids are having all the fun." She was ready for a change.

apprentice: someone who works for another person in order to learn a skill or trade, like pottery or carpentry

6

Loving Clay and Silver

In 1943, Mary, Leo, and Emma sold their Milwaukee home and moved to the house on Beach Drive along Lake Michigan. A short while later, Mary put an end to her teaching career. She was ready to try making a living as an artist. Her interest in pottery **flourished**. She mixed clay in the bathtub and tracked the messy clay dust everywhere. Emma and Leo happily allowed her to move all the pottery work to the basement. Her parents were not fond of Mary's art, but they always encouraged her efforts. They often said, "Well, if it makes Mary happy."

Leo suggested that Mary start a pottery shop. Mary designed a cement block

Ceramic salt and pepper shakers

flourished: grew and succeeded

38

building and Leo made plans to have it built for Mary about
a mile from their house. He would do anything to help his
daughter.

Excited about this plan, Mary worked in the basement
creating pieces of pottery for the shop. First, she did drawings.
Then she made plaster molds. By pouring liquid clay into a
mold, then baking each piece in a kiln, she produced hundreds
of each of her designs.
She worked hard, day
after day, to produce
thousands of pieces
of pottery. She made
whimsical little figures
with big eyes that she
called "**spooks**." She
created vases in many
shapes and sizes—a
woman's head with
a dish on top, a lamp
covered with tiny

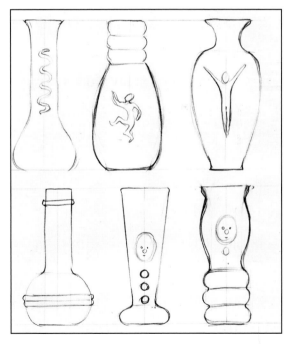

Mary drew many designs before deciding which
to make in clay.

whimsical: playfully creative   spook: a ghost

Stacked clay pieces are ready to fire in the kiln.

faces. She made many playful animals. She also created useful things such as bowls, cups, plates, and candleholders.

In February of 1947, when the building was almost finished, Mary hung out the sign she had painted. It said, "Mary Nohl Ceramics." The special kiln for **firing** the clay arrived in March. In April Mary completed the first firing of her clay work in the new kiln. When the pottery pieces cooled, she arranged them in the **display window** for customers to admire. She admired them too. Horses standing on their back legs, dragons with curled tails, a variety of mugs, and tiny vases filled the shelves. She looked around the shop and sighed with satisfaction. Her dream had come true.

firing: using a lot of heat, as from a fire or kiln, to bake and harden clay   **display window**: a window in the front of a business that shows what's for sale

Mary's building had a shop in front and a **studio** where she could work in back.

Once the shop was open, Mary kept a strict **schedule**, working every day from 9 to 5 with her dog Pooh beside her.

Mary was excited about the pottery studio and shop. She had great hopes for success but crowds of customers did not come to buy. "I wish I knew how

Using molds, Mary could make many copies of each design.

studio: a room where an artist works   **schedule** (**skej** ul): a plan or list of events

to find a pottery **public**. They are certainly coming slowly," she complained in her diary. Her good friend Ros had moved back to Wisconsin. She offered to help with sales. She and Mary piled boxes of pottery into Mary's car and drove to **florists** and gift shops to sell the pottery. Mary did not like selling her work, so she stayed in the car to nap while Ros talked to the owners. Eventually they were able to sell Mary's pottery at stores in 7 states, including Wisconsin.

Even so, sales were not good. Mary became **discouraged**. She sold some pottery at art and craft sales. She also gave lessons to earn money—8 lessons for 8 dollars. But she grew tired of this. "It's funny how I go up and down in this pottery business. When I'm down it's not too bad though—because I know I'll be up again before too long," she told her diary. "I wonder when I'll meet with real success."

What she liked best was thinking up things to create and working with her hands in the pottery studio. She also liked figuring out clever ways to make things. She made her own clay tools and other **equipment**. She was an artist, not a salesperson.

---

public: a community or group of people   **florist**: someone who arranges and sells flowers and plants   **discouraged**: saddened and disappointed   **equipment** (eek **wip** muhnt): tools and machines needed or used for a particular purpose

Mary designed her building so she could both create and sell pottery.

Besides her love of pottery, Mary also got excited about painting. In November 1952, she set up a little area in her pottery studio for painting. She used watercolor and oil paint. "My pottery (studio) has the **turpentine stench** now," she said about her new interest. Turpentine has a strong smell. It is used to clean brushes and make paint thinner and easier

turpentine: a clear liquid made from the sap of pine trees and used to thin paint **stench**: a strong and unpleasant smell

to use. When Mary's parents made their weekly visit to the pottery studio, Mary hid her paints. She was afraid they would smell the turpentine. She didn't want her parents to think that she wasn't paying attention to the pottery business.

Mary kept the shop and studio for 10 years. She never had great success with sales, but she was successful in creating a great amount of pottery. When she decided to close the shop, she packed thousands of pottery pieces into wooden apple boxes. She moved them to the basement at North Beach Drive. Her interests were expanding beyond pottery.

Mary stored extra ceramic pieces in her basement. She gave them away as prizes at card games and as birthday gifts.

Mary knew other artists, but she enjoyed working alone. In the summer of 1950 an artist friend convinced Mary to attend the **Oxbow** Summer School in **Saugatuck**, Michigan. Adult students came from all over the country. They stayed in old cabins in a peaceful, wooded setting and took a variety of art classes. Mary took a **landscape painting** class and **silver working** with Robert **Von Neumann**. He was an outstanding teacher and a well-known Wisconsin artist.

The weeks at Oxbow were joyous and creative. She liked working with silver. When she returned home, she bought equipment for making silver jewelry. She set up a little work area in the house and focused on working in silver. Between 1950 and 1960, Mary created 350 pieces of silver jewelry. Most artists who do silver work buy the silver through craft stores. Mary did this, but she also melted down her mother's **antique** silver spoon collection and other silver wedding presents given to her parents. She considered making jewelry a better use for silver than spoons or platters. Mary said, "Silver is my favorite craft material. . . . It is more beautiful than gold . . . and much less expensive to work with."

Oxbow: oks boh   **Saugatuck: saw** guh tuck   **landscape painting**: a type of painting that shows a large area of land from a distance   **silver working**: making things, such as jewelry, out of silver
Von Neumann: von **noy** muhn   **antique** (an **teek**): old and valuable

She made rings, necklaces, **pendants**, earrings, and bracelets. Sometimes she combined silver with **enamel** or with stones from the beach. Mary carved little faces into smooth stones and bound them in silver. The designs in her silver work include boats and waves, fish, floating people, and mermaids. They show Mary's lifelong fascination with Lake Michigan and nature.

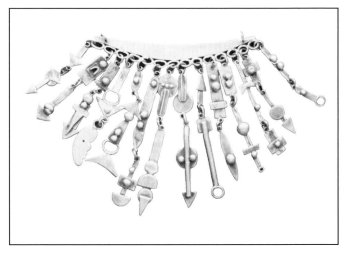

Mary used tiny tools to make fish, people, and intricate designs for this silver necklace.

The boats on Lake Michigan gave Mary the idea for this silver pendant.

pendant: an ornament that hangs from a necklace or bracelet **enamel**: powdered glass that is heated to a high temperature to melt it onto metal, glass, or ceramics

7

Paintings Galore

Mary had the perfect view of Lake Michigan as she painted. She stood at a tall table in a small corner of her upstairs bedroom. Classical music blared from her old Sony radio. The room was cluttered with more than a hundred oil paintings. They were everywhere—on the floor, the bed, and the dresser. Every imaginable space was taken up by Mary's paintings.

She wore her father's old gray sweater. It was covered in swirls and **splotches** of colored paint. The smell of turpentine filled the air. It was winter and the lake was frozen and white. Mary loved painting in the winter. She called it her favorite indoor sport! Often, she lost track of time while she painted. Some days she would paint until the light faded, not even stopping to eat.

splotch: a spot

47

Mary loved to paint but it also frustrated her. One day she liked her paintings and the next day she hated them. She worked and reworked them. When

This is the view of Lake Michigan that Mary saw from her bedroom window.

she decided that one painting needed more white paint, she added white to all the paintings. This allowed Mary to make changes to paintings she hadn't touched for days or weeks or even years.

Mary was excellent at drawing and composition but found working with color to be her biggest challenge. She kept changing the colors. She would add more red to the background only to change it minutes later to gray. The gray would then change to green and so on.

Mary gave a lot of thought to **blending** color. She was never satisfied and never felt her paintings were finished. She didn't put a date on them. She felt that when she **dated** a painting that meant it was complete.

Art school had trained Mary in many ways, but as an adult she painted from her imagination. The figures in her paintings are **eerie**. They are neither

Mary did not title most of her paintings. What title would you give to this?

male nor female. Many are long and skinny. Some look like ghosts. Still others look like swimming fish. Some wear oval masks. Many are missing noses, eyes, and lips. They move or

blending: mixing colors so that they shade into each other little by little   **dated**: put a date on something
eerie: strange or spooky

Figures hover under water. Are they human or are they fish?

float in groups. Some dance in a sea of blue, red, and yellow. The figures are together but they never touch and they never look at each other. Some ride in boats. Others float through buildings and still others look as though they are wandering in a maze. Her images, like her colors, are original and unique.

Mary said about the people in her paintings, "They are people I see every day. People I have known all my life." But was she really painting her family and friends? Who are they? Mary did not like to talk about her art. She never told anyone what she was trying to say in her paintings. All we can do is guess.

During the time Mary was becoming an artist, an art style called **Surrealism** was popular. Surrealist artists painted fantasy pictures from their imagination or **subconscious mind**. Many

Surrealism (suh **ree** uh liz uhm): an art style that combines fantastic and dream-like images
subconscious mind: the part of the mind you aren't aware of but that still has thoughts and feelings

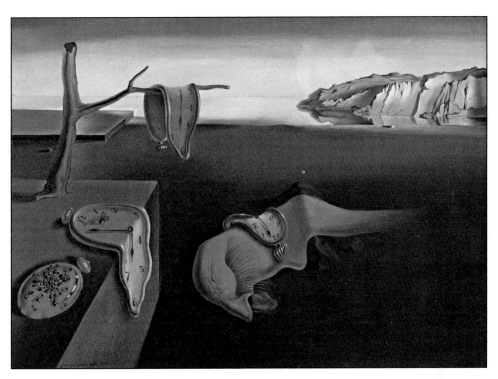

Salvador Dalí was a famous surrealist artist. He painted *The **Persistence** of Memory* in 1931, and it now hangs in the Museum of Modern Art in New York. Why do you think it had that title?

artists painted scenes that look like they come from dreams. Mary's paintings have these **characteristics**. She studied art during the time of this movement. It is possible that the Surrealist painters influenced her.

persistence: continuing   **characteristic** (ker ic tuh **ris** tik): a typical part or quality

Mary often blended the colors with her fingers.

Mary created thousands of paintings during her lifetime. Many were 24 inches tall and 36 inches wide, and they were painted on **Masonite** board. In all of them, there is a similar color and style. Many have familiar images, like fish, people, and boats. Often, they are floating in a dreamlike sea of color.

Mary didn't always paint floating figures. Throughout her life she painted realistic scenes, too. She painted from real, live **models** and set up still-life compositions. She entered painting contests and won many ribbons. Sometimes she used watercolors and sometimes **casein**, but she loved oil painting the best.

Throughout her adult life, Mary kept a strict daily schedule. Every hour of every day was planned. For Mary to accomplish as much as she did, she had to be **disciplined**.

Masonite: wood that has been broken apart and reformed so that it is smooth and hard   **model**: a person who stands or sits so that an artist can draw him or her   **casein** (kay **seen**): a type of paint that is made from milk **disciplined**: controlled in the way you act or behave

Every night before she went to bed she organized the next day. Exercise for 30 minutes, guitar playing for one hour, 8 lines of diary writing, oil painting for 3 hours, yard cleanup, and meal planning were her everyday activities. She kept lists and charts of her **accomplishments**. In the summer months her schedule was even longer. At night she fell into bed exhausted from her full days. Mary also planned social activities. She played on a volleyball team in the summer and in a bowling

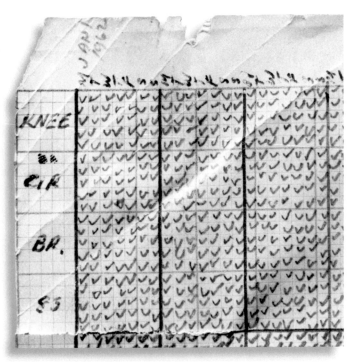

Mary kept track of her daily exercise with this chart. Each check shows an exercise that Mary completed.

league in the winter. She played **bridge** at the Woman's Club of Wisconsin and was friendly with her neighbors. Mary also

accomplishment: an act completed with success   **league** (leeg): an organized group of sports clubs or teams
bridge: a type of card game for 4 players

loved to read. Every 2 weeks she checked a pile of books out of the Fox Point Public Library. Mary had a full and busy life.

How was Mary able to live so well without making a lot of money? The Nohl family was wealthy. Leo was a successful lawyer. His wise **investments** and **thrifty** ways made him a rich man. Mary was grateful for her comfortable life. "I see no reason to not do creative work all the time since I do not need money," Mary wrote in her diary. She was thankful her parents were so generous. She was pleased that they did not **interfere** with what she did.

Like Leo and Emma, Mary was also thrifty. She saved everything, just as her parents did. Her discovery of the village dump in 1949 was a great find. "It's too wonderful what you can find out there!" she wrote. She gathered old rolls of wallpaper, rope, twine, wooden boards, and dishes. She could not resist anything that was free. These found objects might be useful someday, she thought, or they might be helpful to her art. She stored it all in the basement and looked forward to what she would do next.

investment: something purchased with the hope that it will make additional money   **thrifty**: not spending much money   **interfere**: get in the way of

Mary's Adventures around the World

Mary was fortunate to be able to travel somewhere once or twice a year. Wherever she went, Mary had her sketchbook and pencils in hand. Drawing was her way of remembering. Sometimes she sat on a bench in a busy town

Curious children watch Mary on a trip to Mexico in 1936.

square or on a stone wall near an old castle. People gathered around to watch as the scenes appeared on paper before their eyes. She drew women wearing lovely **saris** in India, men wearing **turbans** in Iran and **serapes** and **sombreros** in Mexico. Old **ruins**, cemeteries and beautiful buildings were also favorite subjects. She drew old barns and houses in northern Wisconsin and in the Upper Peninsula of Michigan. She sketched the famous ancient ruins of **Pompeii**, Italy, and the magnificent architecture in Peru and Cambodia.

sari (**sahr** ee): a long piece of light fabric worn wrapped around the body and over one shoulder   **turban**: a long scarf worn wrapped around the head   **serape** (suh **rah** pee): a colorful blanket worn over the shoulders by men in Mexico   **sombrero** (som **brer** oh): a hat whose wide brim helps block the sun   **ruins**: old buildings that are broken-down or destroyed   **Pompeii** (pom **pay**): an ancient city destroyed by a volcano in AD 79

Mary and a friendly monkey in Mexico, 1949. Later, she got 2 monkeys as pets.

Mary traveled all over the world on ships like the Normandie. *She also traveled on trains, in cars, on a raft, and even in a **dugout canoe**.*

Mary made drawings in many corners of the world. She once said, "Just sketching with a pencil opens up a world of ideas and possibilities." She meant that what she drew gave her ideas and inspired the artwork she created at home. All artists find ideas in the world around them. Mary's sculpture, paintings, jewelry, and ceramics show the influence of her travels.

On Easter Island, Mary saw enormous heads **chiseled** from volcanic rock by prehistoric people. She would always remember

dugout canoe: a boat made out of a hollow tree trunk   **chiseled** (**chiz** uhld): cut carefully using sharp tools and a hammer

56

these haunting images. One day they would influence her to create similar sculptures in her own yard. She traveled to **Nepal**, India, **Afghanistan**, Iran, Pakistan, Egypt, and **Trinidad**. In a dugout canoe, she paddled and camped along the Amazon River in South America. She mailed a postcard about this trip to her beloved dogs, **Basil** and Sass. "We had a **first class** adventure in the jungle—like no trip I've ever taken."

When she was too old to travel, Mary could still enjoy her memories by looking through the sketchbooks and travel journals she had created.

The stone heads on Easter Island weigh 20 tons!

How does Mary's concrete head compare to the stone heads on Easter Island?

Nepal: nuh **pawl**   **Afghanistan**: af **gan** uh stan   **Trinidad**: **trin** uh dad   **Basil**: **bay** zuhl   **first class**: the best or highest quality

8

Inside Mary's House

When Mary was a young woman, she often thought about making creative changes to the family's house. But decorating decisions weren't up to her. Perhaps her childhood memories of forts and play houses inspired her desire to **make over** the house on Beach Drive. Her mother always kept the house neat and tidy. **Portraits** of their **ancestors** hung on the walls. The furniture, passed down from Emma's family, was old and dark. Mary loved and respected her mother and her wishes but she had her own ideas about what a house should look like. She wrote in her diary, "[I] keep thinking about all the changes I'll make around the house when I am free to do so."

After Leo died at the age of 87 in 1961, Mary and her mother lived alone in the house. Then Emma grew old and ill. In 1964 she entered a **nursing home**. For 4 years, Mary visited

make over: arrange or form in a new way   **portrait**: a painting or photograph of a person   **ancestor**: a family member from long ago   **nursing home**: a place for the care of the very old or of anyone who needs nursing care over a long period of time

her every day. She played her guitar and brought her mother flowers, ice cream, and cookies for treats. Emma died in 1968.

A new **phase** of life opened to Mary. Now she lived alone. She could change the house any way she liked. She had made small changes while Emma was still at home, but now Mary could do anything—and she did! She was excited to get started. But where should she begin? Mary wrote,"[I] can't decide which part of the house to work on. [There are] so many things to be done."

Everything in every room of the house began to show the touch of Mary's hand. She threw away old things or **donated** them to those in need.

Mary looked at her blank walls and her imagination went wild. She wanted color! She started out slowly by painting bright **turquoise** on the inside of the garage doors, where only she could see it. As she grew **bolder**, Mary whirled red paint on the stairway carpet. She painted the antique furniture in bright colors—red, violet, and light blue. She painted some chairs and a music box red. She painted the bed lavender and

phase: a stage or period of time   **donated**: gave   **turquoise**: tur koiz   **bolder**: more brave

the crystal **chandelier** silver. The little house came alive with color. She wrote in her diary that the people who owned the paint store knew her by name because she bought so much paint.

Mary decorated everything in the living room. Is there anything she missed?

chandelier (shan duh **lir**): a big light fixture that hangs from the ceiling and has many small lights

Soon every surface danced with color. She painted the old telephone with its round **dial** in white and bright red. She even painted a **reclining** woman on the inside of the bathtub! To paint the ceilings she made a special brush by

Pieces of Mary's old fence decorate the fireplace. Heads carved from driftwood rest on the mantle.

dial: the round piece on the front of old phones that was used to select numbers   **reclining**: lying back in a comfortable way

attaching a piece of carpet to a mop handle. She dabbed with this long brush to cover all the walls and ceilings in a pattern of splotches. She used color combinations of black over red, red over turquoise, and light blue and black over white. She painted the stair railing red and carved 41 little wooden spook figures and fish to dangle between the posts of the railing. On the rugs, she swirled black paint in energetic swoops, drips, and dabs. A few years later Mary brightened her clothes by painting them with similar swirls and splashes. Black paint on her red coat, red sweatshirt, and lime green **bell-bottom** pants created quite an outfit!

Mary with her dogs, Icky and Pooh, in 1973. Mary gave her dogs lots of attention and good care. They even went with her to the bank, where they got dog treats.

bell-bottom: pant legs that get wider at the bottom, like a bell

62

With squares of **linoleum** in turquoise and gray, Mary arranged **geometric** patterns on the floor. Chunks of glass, rescued from the dump and glued on the windows, looked like brilliant jewels when the sun shone.

From morning to night, an unending stream of ideas kept Mary busy. She always had more ideas than time. She cut out shapes of fish from **aluminum** food trays and made **mobiles** to hang and spin from the ceilings. She also built **dioramas**. These small wooden boxes displayed little scenes of dancing figures made from wood and clay. Mary said the little boxes reminded her of the dioramas she had seen as a child at the Milwaukee Public Museum. Mary saved chicken bones from her meals and glued them on the kitchen cupboard in the shape of human skeletons. She cut a 3-foot-long snake out of wood to decorate the fireplace. With pieces of wire, she wove large and small human figures, including a cowboy on a horse and a man. These found their places hanging from the ceiling. She **embellished** every corner of the house.

---

linoleum (luh **noh** lee uhm): a material that is often used to cover kitchen floors   **geometric** (jee uh **met** rik): having to do with shapes   **aluminum**: uh **loo** muh nuhm   **mobile** (**moh** beel): a moving sculpture with many different items hanging from wires or strings   **diorama** (dl uh **ram** uh): a lifelike scene made with small figures and other details and a painted background that makes it look real   **embellished**: decorated

Mary used many different materials. Just like when she was a child she loved to find **cast-off** materials that might seem like junk to others. These became

Mary cut out fish from old food trays she had saved. They spin and twirl from the chandelier.

useful for creating sculptures and decorating her house. The lake gave her an endless supply of smooth stones and pieces of driftwood. She created sculptures with big driftwood planks by drilling them with holes and placing plastic animals inside. She hung them on the walls of the stairwell. She said, "I couldn't live without all the things that keep washing up on the beach."

On her daily walks, she discovered all sorts of useful things. She found old keys, sticks, feathers, dried-out pens, fishhooks,

cast-off: thrown away because no one wants it

Mary kept her collections neatly organized in her basement.

and bottle caps. Rusty tools, rope, plastic combs, and empty **spools** were only a few of the items in her collection. She stored all of her found treasures in the basement. There was a box for each category: plastic toys in one box, rubber balls

spool: a roller on which thread or wire is wound

65

of every size in another, and old watches and clocks in still another box. There was a box marked "junk" and even a box of boxes! She stored all of this because she knew it would come in handy someday. Mary used everything. She wasted nothing. With her **vibrant** imagination, she could see great possibilities for any piece of junk.

Mary was happy with all the changes she made. She wrote in her diary, "Everything is improving at a great **rate** here." The unusual sculptures, the fanciful figures, and color everywhere created an amazing sight. People outside the gate could only imagine the inside of Mary's house. What would her mother and father have thought about Mary's decorating style?

vibrant: full of energy and enthusiasm   **rate**: pace

9

Outside Mary's House

Imagine walking down Beach Drive late at night on a summer's evening with a full moon shining on Lake Michigan. As you come to the turn in the road you see something you weren't expecting. At first you are scared and then you are curious. You peer through the wire fence. You can't believe your eyes. In a dark forest of trees are the most amazing animal-like creatures. They stare at you with glass eyes. A huge dinosaur-like creature with a wide-open mouth catches your attention. As you look closer you notice many huge heads staring back at you. The wind blows ever so slightly and you swear you see something move in the trees. A light comes on in the house and you see an old woman in the window on the second floor. She opens the window and your heart is pounding and you scream and run for your life. You saw the witch and you're pretty sure she saw you, too!

That is how many stories about "the witch's house" began. But the real story of "the witch's house" had started many years before.

It took Mary about 30 years to create the magical and mysterious outdoor environment around her house on the shores of Lake Michigan. It started out slowly. One of the first pieces of art that Mary created for her yard was a beautiful blue gate. She cut shapes of fish, boats, and people out of wood. She put the pieces together like a puzzle. The blue gate is important because Mary used these same shapes in many of her art creations. You can see them in her paintings, jewelry, and pottery. Mary made several fences like the blue gate. She called some her "friends and people" fences. They were cutout wood shapes of people and faces in **profile**. She also made some very unusual figures out of tree trunks. She carved them using a chain saw. What a sight that must have been!

These wooden creations are no longer in the yard because they were easy to steal. Kids would come to Mary's house late at night and take a piece of her fence. They even cut down

profile: a view of the side of something

her tree trunk sculptures. So Mary decided to take down the wood fences. She hung some of the wooden people in the trees and others she attached to her house using glue

The blue gates to the yard stood next to stone pillars. Mary and her father made the gateposts when Mary was 12.

and nails. The yard changed many times over the years.

More than 50 concrete sculptures fill the yard that faces the lake. How did Mary make all of those sculptures? First, she used wire and wood to create an **armature** in the shape of the sculpture. Then she dragged an old wheelbarrow that she found at the village dump down to the beach and loaded it up with sand. She hauled it back up to her yard and mixed **limestone**, water, and cement into the sand to make concrete. She worked quickly, often making 10 trips back and forth to

armature (ahr muh chur): framework or structure used to support parts of a sculpture as the artist works on it
limestone: a hard rock used in building and making cement

69

the beach for more sand. When the concrete was ready, Mary added it to the armature. She decorated the sculptures with stones, beach glass, or other found objects.

Some of the sculptures are of whimsical animals. Happy dogs, talking fish, and stony dinosaur-like creatures are placed in **inviting** spaces.

Mary was proud of the fence she made. **Vandals** stole hundreds of pieces but she found other ways to use the pieces they left behind. Can you see them in any of the other photographs in this book?

Many of the sculptures are of people. There are men with fish, children sitting on a bench, groups of people, and figures all alone. There are tall figures wearing crowns, and short heads wearing **derby** hats. There are small heads stacked on top of one another and other heads that form a fence.

vandal: someone who destroys or damages beautiful or valuable things on purpose   derby: a type of hat with a round dome on top and a narrow brim   inviting: making you feel welcome

When vandals burned a wood sculpture in the front yard, Mary and her friends replaced the sculpture with this one of a tall creature with stone teeth.

Mary would never say who these people were, but some of them looked like her father. Some may have been children she knew or wished she knew. They were her imaginary friends and family. When she was working, neighbors stopped to talk and some even offered to help. Mary was creating a strange and wonderful sight on the shores of Lake Michigan.

Mary was **driven** to create. Every day she had a new idea for her yard. One summer she made more than 1,000 square tiles decorated with stones from the beach. She made paths all around her yard with these tiles. Another year she made a pet

driven: really wanting to do something

cemetery. Each dog had its own tombstone!

Mary's travels were a source of inspiration. She often drew old buildings and ruins. In 1969 Mary traveled to Italy. She was fascinated with the buried city of Pompeii. Fifteen feet of ash from a nearby volcano covered the city for 1,700 years! The ash **preserved** the city and

This sculpture looks like the groups of schoolchildren who visited Mary.

when researchers began to uncover it everyone was amazed at what they found. Mary drew many sketches of the ruins. When she returned to her home, she created a miniature Pompeii in her yard.

preserved: protected so that something stays in its original state

At the same time she was making sculptures in the yard Mary began to decorate the outside of the house. She hung little driftwood heads above her front door and attached

Each man faces a different direction and has a different expression.

driftwood stick men to the house to embellish the little wood cottage. She nailed and glued cutout figures around the frames of her windows, and painted them in bright reds and blues. She added a huge wooden red fish skeleton to one side of the house and then added a similar one to the other side.

The possibilities were endless. The more Mary created, the more ideas she had for art inside her house and outside in her yard. Her energy was boundless. She was a true artist.

Rumors about Mary began to spread. Carloads of teens and adults drove to her house from all over Milwaukee. People were curious. Who was this woman? Some people said that she was a witch. Others said she drowned her children in the lake and that's why she made the sculptures of children. Some said she was mean and had a gun. Of course, none of these rumors were true. Mary was a creative woman who made art her life.

She had many fans. Mary treasured the letters, poems, drawings, and notes that were left in her mailbox. She was happy to show visitors around her yard if she had the time. She loved the schoolchildren who came to visit. At times, however, she avoided visitors. The attention was more than Mary could handle.

rumor: a story or opinion that people tell each other, passing it on without knowing if it is true or not

Mary wears her favorite outfit, which she painted, and a silver necklace she made.

A Tour of the Yard

The tour of Mary's yard starts at the front gate. In 1926 Mary and her father collected sand and rocks from the beach and mixed the concrete to form 2 gateposts. Today 2 smiling sculptures sit on top of these posts. These happy faces greet you as you walk or drive by.

One of the faces at the top of Mary's gatepost.

Inside the yard, a path of stone tiles Mary made leads you around the house. A dog that looks like a dinosaur sits waiting to welcome visitors. He is about 4 feet tall and 4 feet long. Beach pebbles form his face and coat. He has glass eyes and a big toothy grin. He is just tall enough that you can reach out and pet his stone head. As you walk on the path toward the front steps you realize that the yard is an amazing place.

The front of Mary's house. Mary's bedroom was on the second floor on the left.

A smiling creature with stone teeth greets visitors.

The stone creatures are enchanting and fanciful. Just past the smiling dog is a man with a large seated fish on his lap. They seem to be having a serious conversation. To the right, a smiling man with a funny hat is surrounded by dozens of large standing fish. Looking toward the lake you notice many large concrete heads. Standing more than 8 feet tall, they stare at you with glass eyes. Some heads have large chins that stick out, while others have long wide noses. Some heads come to a point at the top and others wear a glass crown or a concrete hat. Still others have concrete spikes for hair. You wonder who these mysterious people are.

A life-size concrete man hugs a fish.

The front door is painted a turquoise blue with a blue hand as a doorknocker. If you look up you will notice driftwood heads bobbing above you. If you look down you will see the word "BOO" spelled out with black stones on the doorstep. The house itself is enhanced with hundreds of cutout images of fish, people,

Mary carved this 6-finger door knocker from wood. It made a very loud sound.

Wooden heads carved from driftwood hang over Mary's front door.

and boats. There is so much to see and take in.

As you head down the path toward the lake you come across a bench where 4 children sit. They look as if they are taking a rest from playing. One child may be unhappy. They have spiky hair and flat faces. Next to them is a seated couple with their arms around each other. Just beyond them is a large dinosaur-like creature with a figure leaning against it. All these statues are made out of concrete. The dinosaur creature is the tallest sculpture in the yard, more than 15 feet tall. He is smiling like the other animals.

On the back of the house, cutout wooden shapes are nailed to the wood siding. These cutouts of fish, people, boats, and spooks are arranged in a beautiful and colorful design. The **side yard** is warm and cozy and is as **intriguing** as the front. The sun shines on the red and blue cutouts on the house. A concrete sculpture of a seated couple welcomes you into the space. A reclining figure fills the center of the courtyard. Mary often came out her kitchen door and ate her lunch in this inviting space.

Mary liked to eat her lunch on the patio next to the kitchen.

side yard: yard at the side of a house   **intriguing**: in **tree** ging

The stone tile path leads you between the Hall of the Mountain King towers. These 10-foot-high sculptures are different from the massive heads and figures of the front yard. Mary dripped concrete to form small heads upon small heads until the sculptures were tall and wide.

If you continue on the path you enter into the wild and overgrown backyard. It's full of big trees and green areas. The only sculptures

The Hall of the Mountain King towers were made of concrete and colored glass chunks. The stone path leads into the woods.

to be found here are hanging in the trees. They are pieces of her "friends and family fence."

The tour of Mary's yard delights visitors of every age. There is so much to see that you need to come back again and again.

10

Leaving the Lakeshore

Driven by her creativity and her love of art, Mary Nohl carved out her own path in life. She taught art, ran a pottery studio, and devoted herself to **transforming** her house and yard. She created hundreds of paintings, pieces of jewelry, pottery, and sculptures. Her hard work resulted in wonderful creations found both inside and outside of her home on the lakeshore. The curious and haunting environment she created is loved by people young and old. Anyone peeping through her fence is touched by the power and magic of her creations.

From a bed in her living room, Mary spent her last days watching her favorite view of Lake Michigan. She never tired of it. The changing colors of the lake and sky and the sound of the waves gave her comfort and a feeling of peace.

transforming: changing into something else

Mary died on December 22, 2001, at the age of 87. She was buried in the Forest Home Cemetery in Milwaukee, where her family and many of the city's well-known people are also buried.

Her old friend, Ros, spoke to a news reporter after Mary's death. She said, "[Mary] did not run in the same **channels** as other people. She did her art the way she wanted it, and didn't care what anyone thought.... She kept creating from morning to night, all the years I knew her."

Mary Nohl's creative life produced 2 meaningful gifts that keep giving even after her death. Her greatest gift is the magical **site** she created on Beach Drive. People come from near and far to gaze and marvel at the unique beauty and mystery of "the witch's house." Mary's creation has received much-deserved recognition. Her property is on the National **Register** of Historic Places and the Wisconsin Register of Historic Places. It also was nominated as a Milwaukee County **Landmark**. After her death, Mary was awarded the Wisconsin

---

channel: a way or course of thinking or acting   **site**: location, place   **register**: official record or list
landmark: a building or place that is seen as especially important

Visual Art Lifetime Achievement Award in 2008. Stories about her appeared in many newspapers and magazines throughout her lifetime and beyond.

Mary's other gift was the money she left to the community of Milwaukee. Mary once said she would like to "do some large project doing good in Milwaukee." The money she had so carefully taken care of became that project. She donated her **estate** to the Greater Milwaukee Foundation. With this money, the foundation created a special **fund** called The Mary L. Nohl Fund. Every year this money helps artists, arts centers, and children who are able to learn about art because of her gift. This fund also provides art school **scholarships** at the Milwaukee Institute of Art and Design and helps with art projects at the Boys' and Girls' Clubs. People in and around Milwaukee are **enriched** by this gift.

In Mary's later years, she worried about what would happen to her house and the works of art she created. The Kohler Foundation preserves art environments like Mary's. They helped Mary and worked closely with her to find a

estate: the money, land, and other belongings that a person leaves behind after dying   **fund**: an amount of money kept for a special purpose   **scholarship** (**skah** ler ship): money given to help a student continue studying   **enriched**: made better or richer

way to preserve her home and art and make it available to the public. Mary donated her art and property to the Kohler Foundation. Many of Mary's wonderful paintings, jewelry, sculptures, and drawings are now part of the **collection** of the John Michael Kohler Arts Center in Sheboygan, where they are cared for and often on display for visitors to see.

Mary's art environment is a treasure for the state of Wisconsin. Mary Nohl will long be remembered because of her creativity and commitment—and a lifetime lived in art.

Mary Nohl loved life *and* art.

collection: all of the art that belongs to a museum

Appendix

Mary's Time Line

1907 — Leo Nohl and Emma Parmenter are married.

1910 — On September 22, Max Nohl is born.

1914 — On September 6, Mary Nohl is born.

1924 — The Nohl family buys one and a half acres of land on the shore of Lake Michigan.

1926 — Mary and her father build gateposts for the Lake Michigan property.

Mary begins writing in a diary.

1928 — On March 24, Mary wins first place for a model-airplane flying contest.

Mary graduates from Hartford Avenue School.

1932 — On June 8, Mary graduates from Milwaukee University School.

1932–1933 — Mary attends Rollins College in Winter Park, Florida.

1933 — Mary starts work on the *Danny Diver* book, which takes her about 5 years to finish.

1933–1937 — Mary attends the Art Institute of Chicago. She graduates on June 11, 1937, with a bachelor of fine arts.

1935 — Mary travels to Europe and visits France, England, Belgium, Switzerland, Italy, Germany, Portugal, and Algiers.

1937 — On December 1, Max Nohl makes a record-breaking deep-water dive in Lake Michigan.

1939 — Mary receives a bachelor of art in education from the Art Institute of Chicago.

Mary moves to Maryland to teach school.

1941 — Mary moves back to her parents' home in Milwaukee.

1941–1942 — Mary teaches briefly at North Division High School in Milwaukee.

1942–1944 — Mary teaches at Steuben Junior High School in Milwaukee.

1943 — Mary begins designing and creating pottery.

The Nohl family moves from their home in Milwaukee to their home on Lake Michigan at Beach Drive.

1947 — Mary's pottery studio and shop are built.

1950 — In June, Mary attends a silver-working class at Oxbow School in Michigan. She produces 350 pieces of silver jewelry over the next 10 years.

1960 — Mary begins painting. Over the next 30 years she creates thousands of paintings.

On February 6, Mary's brother, Max, dies in a car accident.

1961 — On December 6, Leo Nohl, Mary's father, dies.

1963 — Mary begins to create concrete and driftwood sculptures in her yard.

1964 — Emma Nohl, Mary's mother, enters a nursing home.

1968 — On January 20, Emma Nohl dies.

1969 — Thefts from Mary's yard include 2 concrete heads and 50 pieces from her wooden fence. Mary replaces the fence with a chain-link fence to prevent vandalism and stealing.

1996 — Mary gives her house and artwork to the Kohler Foundation for preservation.

2001 — On December 22, Mary dies.

2005 — Mary's art environment is listed on the National Register of Historic Places.

2008 — Mary is awarded the Wisconsin Visual Art Lifetime Achievement Award.

Appendix

Gallery of Mary's Art

Mary as a college student with a pen and sketchbook.
Rolled-down stockings were the style then.

Mary liked sleeping out in a tent or on an old mattress when she was young.

How would you describe these figures?

This tiny silver book was part of a ring you could put on your finger. The pages moved.

The boats on Lake Michigan inspired Mary to make this silver pendant.

Do you see a similarity between this painting and Mary's pendant on page 91?

What was in Mary's mind when she painted these floating figures?

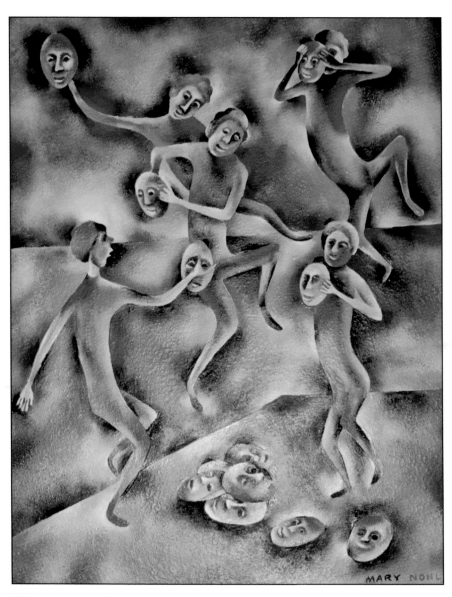

What story would you tell about this painting?

The figures Mary painted were mysterious. What do you think they are looking at?

Mary wound and sewed many yards of **jute** to create this life-size floppy figure.

jute (joot): strong, tough fibers or threads from tropical plants that are used to make string

The entry hall of Mary's house

Mary loved to decorate everyday objects in
her home, like this old-fashioned phone.

Every wall, ceiling, and surface shows Mary's work.

Mary's front yard attracted a lot of attention!

Mary had a sense of humor. She made the concrete fish sit on a bench like people.

How many fish do you think this statue is holding?

This concrete head faces the lake.

These sun-faced figures face up, and the hooded figure looks down. Vandals broke the heads off these concrete sculptures. Later they were repaired.

A friendly couple in concrete

This life-size driftwood man hangs
beside the front door.

Glossary

Pronunciation Key

a   cat (kat), plaid (plad),
half (haf)

ah   father (**fah** THur),
heart (hahrt)

air   carry (**kair** ee), bear (bair),
where (whair)

aw   all (awl), law (law),
bought (bawt)

ay   say (say), break (brayk),
vein (vayn)

e   bet (bet), says (sez),
deaf (def)

ee   bee (bee), team (teem),
fear (feer)

i   bit (bit), women (**wim** uhn),
build (bild)

ɪ   ice (ɪs), lie (lɪ), sky (skɪ)

o   hot (hot), watch (wotch)

oh   open (**oh** puhn), sew (soh)

oi   boil (boil), boy (boi)

oo   pool (pool), move (moov),
shoe (shoo)

or   order (**or** dur), more (mor)

ou   house (hous), now (nou)

u   good (gud), should (shud)

uh   cup (kuhp), flood (fluhd),
button (**buht** uhn)

ur   burn (burn), pearl (purl),
bird (burd)

yoo   use (yooz), few (fyoo),
view (vyoo)

hw   what (hwuht), when (hwen)

TH   that (THat), breathe (breeTH)

zh   measure (**mezh** ur),
garage (guh **razh**)

accomplishment: an act completed with success

adventuresome: willing to go on an adventure

ancestor: a family member from long ago

antique (an **teek**): old and valuable

apprentice: someone who works for another person in order to learn a skill or trade, like pottery or carpentry

armature (**ahr** muh chur): framework or structure used to support parts of a sculpture as the artist works on it

awkward: clumsy

balsa (**bawl** suh): a really light wood that comes from a tropical tree

bell-bottom: pant legs that get wider at the bottom, like a bell

blending: mixing colors so that they shade into each other little by little

bolder: more brave

bridge: a type of card game for 4 players

capsized: tipped over

capsule (**kap** suhl): a container

cargo ship: a ship that carries goods like salt, wheat, or lumber

Caribbean (cair ruh **bee** uhn or cair **ri** bee uhn): the sea between North and South America

casein (kay **seen**): a type of paint that is made from milk

cast-off: thrown away because no one wants it

cathedral (kuh **thee** druhl): a large church

ceramics (ser **a** miks): pottery

chandelier (shan duh **lir**): a big light fixture that hangs from the ceiling and has many small lights

channel: a way or course of thinking or acting

characteristic (ker ic tuh **ris** tik): a typical part or quality

chiseled (**chiz** uhld): cut carefully using sharp tools and a hammer

cigar band: a loop of paper or foil wrapped on a cigar that shows its brand

citywide: involving a whole city

collaborated: worked together

collection: all of the art that belongs to a museum

color chart: a piece of paper with squares of different colors on it, used to check colors and make sure they are correct and go well together

compass: a tool with 2 legs and a movable joint, used for drawing circles and arcs

concrete: a building material made up of sand, gravel, cement, and water that becomes very hard when it dries

dated: put a date on something

derby: a type of hat with a round dome on top and a narrow brim

descent (di **sent**): from a certain country or culture

device: a piece of equipment that does a particular job

dial: the round piece on the front of old phones that was used to select numbers

diorama (dɪ uh **ram** uh): a lifelike scene made with small figures and other details and a painted background that makes it look real

disciplined: controlled in the way you act or behave

discouraged: saddened and disappointed

display window: a window in the front of a business that shows what's for sale

donated: gave

driftwood: wood that has spent a long time floating in a lake or ocean and is sometimes washed up on shore

drive: a longing or need to do something

driven: really wanting to do something

dugout canoe: a boat made out of a hollow tree trunk

Easter Island: an island in the Pacific Ocean

eerie: strange or spooky

egg tempera: a type of paint that uses the white part of an egg mixed with color

embellished: decorated

enamel: powdered glass that is heated to a high temperature to melt it onto metal, glass, or ceramics

enriched: made better or richer

entry: a piece of information in a book such as a diary or dictionary

environment (en **vi** ruhn muhnt): a place and its surroundings

equipment (eek **wip** muhnt): tools and machines needed or used for a particular purpose

estate: the money, land, and other belongings that a person leaves behind after dying

exotic: strange and interesting

exploration: studying or discovering an unknown thing

fascinating: very interesting

figure: a shape or outline

figure drawing: drawing of the human body

firing: using a lot of heat, as from a fire or kiln, to bake and harden clay

first class: the best or highest quality

florist: someone who arranges and sells flowers and plants

flourished: grew and succeeded

found object: something that wasn't made to be art but that an artist takes and uses in a new artistic way

fund: an amount of money kept for a special purpose

geometric (jee uh **met** rik): having to do with shapes

graduated (**graj** oo ay tud): finished school

Great Depression: the decade of the 1930s when many people in the United States had no jobs and were very poor

hitchhiked: got rides in strangers' cars by standing on the side of the road and waiting for someone to stop

hobbyhorse: a child's toy made of a stick with a fake horse's head on one end

home economics class: class where skills like sewing and cooking are taught

India ink: a special type of dark black ink

influence: the ability to get someone to think or behave in a certain way

institute (**in** stuh toot): a building or organization with a specific goal

interfere: get in the way of

intruder: a person who goes into a place without permission

investment: something purchased with the hope that it will make additional money

inviting: making you feel welcome

jute (joot): strong, tough fibers or threads from tropical plants that are used to make string

keen: eager, enthusiastic

kiln: a very hot oven used to bake and harden clay

landmark: a building or place that is seen as especially important

landscape painting: a type of painting that shows a large area of land from a distance

league (leeg): an organized group of sports clubs or teams

lecture: give a talk to an audience, often at a college or university

lettering: the art of drawing and writing the letters of the alphabet in special ways, such as for a sign or a greeting card

limestone: a hard rock used in building and making cement

linoleum (luh **noh** lee uhm): a material that is often used to cover kitchen floors

make over: arrange or form in a new way

Masonite: wood that has been broken apart and reformed so that it is smooth and hard

mature (muh **chur**): become more grown up

mechanical drawing: a drawing made with rulers and compasses

mobile (**moh** beel): a moving sculpture with many different items hanging from wires or strings

model: a person who stands or sits so that an artist can draw him or her

mysterious (mi **stir** ee uhs): hard to understand or explain

nursing home: a place for the care of the very old or of anyone who needs nursing care over a long period of time

oil paint: a type of paint that uses oil mixed with color

pendant: an ornament that hangs from a necklace or bracelet

perch: sit or stand on the edge of something

persistence: continuing

petroleum (puh **troh** lee uhm) **jelly**: an oily substance often used in medicines and makeup

phase: a stage or period of time

pint (pɪnt): a small container

plaster mold: a container in a particular shape, which makes anything poured into it, when dried, into that shape

Pompeii (pom **pay**): an ancient city destroyed by a volcano in AD 79

portrait: a painting or photograph of a person

pottery: containers made of wet clay that is then hardened in a hot oven

prank: a playful trick

preserved: protected so that something stays in its original state

profile: a view of the side of something

propel: move something forward

public: a community or group of people

put down her roots: made someplace her home and became connected to it

rate: pace

reclining: lying back in a comfortable way

register: official record or list

reuse: use again

ruins: old buildings that are broken-down or destroyed

rumor: a story or opinion that people tell each other, passing it on without knowing if it is true or not

sari (**sahr** ee): a long piece of light fabric worn wrapped around the body and over one shoulder

schedule (**skej** ul): a plan or list of events

scholarship (**skah** ler ship): money given to help a student continue studying

self-confidence: belief in one's abilities and worth

self-conscious (self **kon** shuhs): worried about how you look to other people

sensation: feeling

serape (suh **rah** pee): a colorful blanket worn over the shoulders by men in Mexico

shop class: class where skills like carpentry are taught

short-sheet: to fold and tuck the sheets on someone's bed so that they can't get all the way in

side yard: yard at the side of a house

silver working: making things, such as jewelry, out of silver

site: location, place

sketch: a simple drawing

social life: the time you spend having fun with friends

sombrero (som **brer** oh): a hat whose wide brim helps block the sun

splotch: a spot

spook: a ghost

spool: a roller on which thread or wire is wound

stench: a strong and unpleasant smell

still-life composition: a painting or drawing of objects that aren't moving

stocking: a pair of thin, delicate tights that are easily torn

strict: making sure all the rules are followed

studio: a room where an artist works

subconscious mind: the part of the mind you aren't aware of but that still has thoughts and feelings

suburb: homes and shopping centers beyond the main settled areas of a city

Surrealism (suh **ree** uh liz uhm): an art style that combines fantastic and dream-like images

suspended: attached to something and hanging downward

technology (tek **nol** uh jee): the use of science to do practical things

thrifty: not spending much money

transforming: changing into something else

trolley car: a type of car that runs on tracks on a city street and is powered by electricity

turban: a long scarf worn wrapped around the head

turpentine: a clear liquid made from the sap of pine trees and used to thin paint

unique (yoo **neek**): the only one of its kind

vandal: someone who destroys or damages beautiful or valuable things on purpose

vibrant: full of energy and enthusiasm

watercolor: a type of paint that uses water mixed with color

whimsical: playfully creative

Reading Group Guide and Activities

Discussion Questions

❧ Mary Nohl created art from morning to night. Do you ever feel the urge to make things? What do you like to create? What do you think drove Mary to create?

❧ How is your life different from Mary Nohl's life as a child? How is it the same? Can you give some examples of the differences and similarities?

❧ Mary created most of her art in her home on the shores of Lake Michigan, but many of her ideas for art came from her travels. Why do you think Mary's travels inspired her art? Why was it important for her to keep a journal of her travels?

❧ Other than traveling, where did Mary get her ideas for her art? What do you think she found so appealing about making art? Why do you think she used objects other people would throw away?

❧ Mary's house was known as "the witch's house" in the area where she lived. Why do you think this was? Why were there so many rumors about Mary?

Activities

❧ Using papier-mâché and paint, create a whimsical figure like the kind Mary Nohl made. Alternatively, use construction paper pasted to card stock to make colorful cutout shapes of boats, spooks, fish, people, and other objects like those on the outside of Mary's house. Then, set up a gallery of sculptures and cutout figures with your classmates and have an "art show" that others can attend.

- Keep your own diary for one week. Write 8 lines every day. At the end of the week read your diary entries. What have you learned from this experience? What have you learned about yourself? As an alternative, keep a "sketch journal" for one week, making drawings of the things and people in your life.

- Look around your neighborhood for natural or human-made things like those that appealed to Mary Nohl. Imagine how you could reuse these found objects. Choose a few items to bring into class for an art project (but check with an adult to make sure they're safe). Use these objects either to create a piece of artwork or to assemble a piece of jewelry.

- Mary Nohl said that drawing is a good way of remembering. Take a drawing pad and pencil to your playground or a park and draw the scenes that you see around you. Then present your work to your class. What stories do these pictures tell?

- Create a mobile. With a pair of scissors, cut fish and other animal shapes from stiff paper or cardboard. Poke a hole in the top edge of the cutout figure. Insert fishing line or thread through the hole and tie it to a stick. Hang the figures from the stick at different lengths. Arrange the parts so they can move freely in the air without touching each other. Suspend the stick from a high spot.

To Learn More about Being an Artist

Alexander, Kay. *Art Activities with Paper, Clay, Fibers, and Printmaking: Using Masterworks as Inspiration.* Glenview, IL: Crystal Productions, 2011.

Greenberg, Jan, and Sandra Jordan. *The Painter's Eye: Learning to Look at Contemporary American Art.* New York: Delacorte Press, 1991.

Kohl, MaryAnn. *Art with Anything: 52 Weeks of Fun Using Everyday Stuff.* Silver Spring, MD: Gryphon House, 2010.

Nilsen, Anna. *The Great Art Scandal: Solve the Crime, Save the Show.* Boston: Kingfisher, 2003.

Panchyk, Richard. *American Folk Art for Kids: With 21 Activities.* Chicago: Chicago Review Press, 2004.

Schick, Eleanor. *Art Lessons.* New York: Greenwillow Books, 1987.

Sellen, Betty-Carol, with Cynthia Johanson. *Self Taught, Outsider, and Folk Art: A Guide to American Artists, Locations and Resources.* Jefferson, NC: McFarland & Co., 2000.

Sousa, Jean. *Faces, Places and Inner Spaces: A Guide to Looking at Art.* New York: Abrams Books for Young Readers, published in association with The Art Institute of Chicago, 2006.

Acknowledgments

It was a great honor to meet and know Mary Nohl. She was open and generous. She welcomed the idea of our writing her life story. She allowed us to interview and document her life. After her death in 2001 the Kohler Foundation permitted us full access to her materials and provided a grant to use them in this book. We were grateful for this opportunity.

We'd also like to acknowledge the following sources: conversations with Mary Nohl between 1989 and 2001; personal interviews with Rosalind Couture and John Willets; Ruth Kohler and the John Michael Kohler Art Center; Terry Yoho and the Mary Nohl Archive at the Kohler Foundation; and the letters, diaries, sketchbooks, idea books, travel books, photos, scrapbooks, and drawings in the Mary Nohl Archive. In addition, our book *Mary Nohl: Inside & Outside; Biography of the Artist* was helpful.

Illustration Credits

Page viii Mary Nohl Lake Cottage Environment (site detail, Fox Point, Wisconsin), John Michael Kohler Arts Center Collection. Photo: 2007, Janine Smith. **Page 1** Mary Nohl Lake Cottage Environment (site detail, three figures, Fox Point, Wisconsin), John Michael Kohler Arts Center Collection. Photo: ca. 1985–1995, Barbara Manger. **Page 2** Mary Nohl Lake Cottage Environment (site detail, "boo" in stones, Fox Point, Wisconsin), John Michael Kohler Arts Center Collection. Photo: ca. 1989, Barbara Manger. **Page 4** Family portrait, 1915. Courtesy of the John Michael Kohler Arts Center Artist Archives. **Page 5** Stowell Avenue home, 1920. Courtesy of the John Michael Kohler Arts Center Artist Archives. **Page 6** Untitled drawing, age 5, 1918. Courtesy of the John Michael Kohler Arts Center Artist Archives **Page 8** *Her Best Beloved Home,* ca. 1920. Courtesy of the John Michael Kohler Arts Center Artist Archives. **Page 10** *The Wisconsin News.* **Page 12** Amelia Janes, Earth Illustrated, Inc. **Page 14** Selection of diaries, n.d. Courtesy of the John Michael Kohler Arts Center Artist Archives. **Page 17** High school photo, ca. 1930s. Courtesy of the John Michael Kohler Arts Center Artist Archives. **Page 18** Mary painting at Rollins College, 1933. Courtesy of the John Michael Kohler Arts Center Artist Archives. **Page 19** Sketch featuring ceramic casting, 1948. Courtesy of the John Michael Kohler Arts Center Artist Archives. **Page 20** Travel journals, n.d. Courtesy of the John Michael Kohler Arts

Center Artist Archives. **Page 23** Grant Wood, *American Gothic,* 1930, oil on beaver board, 30 3/4 x 25 3/4 inches. Friends of American Art Collection, 1930.934, Gallery 263, The Art Institute of Chicago. **Page 24** Sketchbook drawing, ca. 1930s. Courtesy of the John Michael Kohler Arts Center Artist Archives. **Page 25** Self-portraits, ca. 1933–36. Courtesy of the John Michael Kohler Arts Center Artist Archives. **Page 27** Max and Mary Nohl, 1920. Courtesy of the John Michael Kohler Arts Center Artist Archives. **Page 29** Max Nohl's thesis, 1935, public domain. **Page 30** Max Gene Nohl above Lake Michigan, December 1, 1937. Courtesy of the John Michael Kohler Arts Center Artist Archives. **Page 32** *Danny Diver* comic strip (detail, four-panel excerpt), ca. 1938; ink on paper; 5 x 16 in. John Michael Kohler Arts Center Collection, Gift of Mary Nohl. **Page 33** *Danny Diver* comic strip (detail, four-panel excerpt), ca. 1938; ink on paper; 5 x 16 in. John Michael Kohler Arts Center Collection, Gift of Mary Nohl. **Page 34** Untitled, ca. 1936; gouache and ink on paper; 8 x 9 1/8 in. John Michael Kohler Arts Center Collection. **Page 36** Ros Couture Tubesing and Mary Nohl, 1941. Courtesy of the John Michael Kohler Arts Center Artist Archives. **Page 38** Untitled, 1951; clay and glaze; 13 1/8 x 10 1/8 x 3 1/8 in. John Michael Kohler Arts Center Collection. **Page 39** Sketches of vases, ca. 1948–55. Courtesy of the John Michael Kohler Arts Center Artist Archives. **Page 40** Kiln at Mary Nohl Ceramics, ca. 1947.

Courtesy of the John Michael Kohler Arts Center Artist Archives. **Page 41, top** Mary Nohl Ceramics, ca. 1947. Courtesy of the John Michael Kohler Arts Center Artist Archives. **Page 41, bottom** Mary Nohl Ceramics window, ca. 1948-55. Courtesy of the John Michael Kohler Arts Center Artist Archives. **Page 43** Mary in her pottery studio, ca. 1948. Courtesy of the John Michael Kohler Arts Center Artist Archives. **Page 44** Pottery in the basement of Mary Nohl's home. John Michael Kohler Arts Center Artist Archives. Photo: 2001, Janine Smith. **Page 46** Untitled (necklace), ca. 1949-75; silver; 20 x 1 3/4 x 1/8 in. John Michael Kohler Arts Center Collection, Gift of Mary Nohl. **Page 46** Untitled (pendant), ca. 1949-75; silver; 4 1/2 x 4 1/2 x 1/8 in. John Michael Kohler Arts Center Collection, Gift of Mary Nohl. **Page 48** Mary Nohl Lake Cottage Environment (site detail, view from Mary's bedroom window, Fox Point, Wisconsin), John Michael Kohler Arts Center Collection. Photo: 2007, Janine Smith. **Page 49** Untitled, n.d.; oil on board; 35 7/8 x 23 3/4 in. John Michael Kohler Arts Center Collection, Gift of Mary Nohl. **Page 50** Untitled, n.d.; oil on board; 37 3/4 x 23 5/8 in. John Michael Kohler Arts Center Collection, Gift of Mary Nohl. **Page 51** Salvador Dalí, *The Persistence of Memory.* Oil on canvas, 9 1/2 inches x 13 inches, 1931, The Museum of Modern Art, New York. © Salvador Dalí, Fundació Gala Salvador Dalí, Artists Rights Society (ARS), New York 2012, The Museum of Modern Art, New York, NY, U.S.A. Digital image © The Museum of Modern Art/ Licensed by SCALA/Art Resource, NY. **Page 52** Untitled, n.d.; oil on board; 36 x 23 7/8 in. John Michael Kohler Arts Center Collection, Gift of Mary Nohl. **Page 53** Mary's exercise chart, 1962. Courtesy of the John Michael Kohler Arts Center Artist Archives. **Page 55**

Watercolor from Mary's travel notebook (Mexico), ca. 1936. Courtesy of the John Michael Kohler Arts Center Artist Archives. **Page 56, left** Mary with monkey, 1949. Courtesy of the John Michael Kohler Arts Center Artist Archives. **Page 56, right** Mary on the *Normandie,* 1940. Courtesy of the John Michael Kohler Arts Center Artist Archives. **Page 57, left** Artemio Urbina. **Page 57, right** Mary Nohl Lake Cottage Environment (site detail, stone bust, Fox Point, Wisconsin), John Michael Kohler Arts Center Collection. Photo: 2007, Janine Smith. **Page 60** Mary Nohl Lake Cottage Environment (interior site detail, Fox Point, Wisconsin), John Michael Kohler Arts Center Collection. Photo: 2004, Scott Dietrich. **Page 61** Mary Nohl Lake Cottage Environment (interior site detail, mantel, Fox Point, Wisconsin), John Michael Kohler Arts Center Collection. Photo: 2004, Scott Dietrich. **Page 62** Mary with her dogs Icky and Pooh, 1973. Courtesy of the John Michael Kohler Arts Center Artist Archives. **Page 64** Mary Nohl Lake Cottage Environment (interior site detail, chandelier, Fox Point, Wisconsin), John Michael Kohler Arts Center Collection. Photo: 2007, Janine Smith. **Page 65** Mary Nohl Lake Cottage Environment (interior site detail, supplies hanging in basement, Fox Point, Wisconsin), John Michael Kohler Arts Center Collection. Photo: 2001, Janine Smith. **Page 69** Mary in front of a gate at her home, 1963. Courtesy of the John Michael Kohler Arts Center Artist Archives. **Page 70** A gate at Mary's home, 1973. Courtesy of the John Michael Kohler Arts Center Artist Archives. **Page 71** Mary and friends working on sculpture, 1973. Courtesy of the John Michael Kohler Arts Center Artist Archives. **Page 72** Mary Nohl Lake Cottage Environment (site detail, sculpture group, Fox Point, Wisconsin),

John Michael Kohler Arts Center Collection. Photo: 2007, Janine Smith. **Page 73** Mary Nohl Lake Cottage Environment (site detail, men with hats, Fox Point, Wisconsin), John Michael Kohler Arts Center Collection. Photo: 2007, Janine Smith. **Page75** Mary Nohl at her Lake Cottage Environment. Photo: 1994, Ron Byers. **Page 76, top** Kerri Servis © 2008. **Page 76, bottom** Mary Nohl Lake Cottage Environment (site detail, front gate, Fox Point, Wisconsin), John Michael Kohler Arts Center Collection. Photo: 2007, Janine Smith. **Page 77, top** Mary Nohl Lake Cottage Environment (site detail, Fox Point, Wisconsin), John Michael Kohler Arts Center Collection. Photo: 2008, Janine Smith. **Page 77, bottom** Mary Nohl Lake Cottage Environment (site detail, dinosaur sculpture, Fox Point, Wisconsin), John Michael Kohler Arts Center Collection. Photo: 2008, Janine Smith. **Page 78** Mary Nohl Lake Cottage Environment (site detail, man and fish, Fox Point, Wisconsin), John Michael Kohler Arts Center Collection. Photo: 2007, Janine Smith. **Page 79, left** Mary Nohl Lake Cottage Environment (site detail, front door, Fox Point, Wisconsin), John Michael Kohler Arts Center Collection. Photo: 2007, Janine Smith. **Page 79, inset** Mary Nohl Lake Cottage Environment (site detail, door knocker, Fox Point, Wisconsin), John Michael Kohler Arts Center Collection. Photo: 2007, Janine Smith. **Page 80** Mary Nohl Lake Cottage Environment (site detail, Fox Point, Wisconsin), John Michael Kohler Arts Center Collection. Photo: 2007, Janine Smith. **Page 81** Mary Nohl Lake Cottage Environment (site detail, Fox Point, Wisconsin), John Michael Kohler Arts Center Collection. Photo: 2008, Janine Smith. **Page 85** *Milwaukee Journal Sentinel.* **Page 89** Untitled, ca. 1936; gouache and graphite on paper; 36 x 23 7/8 in. John Michael Kohler

Arts Center Collection, Gift of Mary Nohl. **Page 90** Watercolor from Mary's travel notebook, ca. 1936. Courtesy of the John Michael Kohler Arts Center Artist Archives. **Page 91, top** Untitled (pendant), c. 1949-75; silver; 2 3/4 x 4 x 3/8 in. John Michael Kohler Arts Center Collection, Gift of Mary Nohl. **Page 91, middle** Untitled (ring), ca. 1949-75; silver; 1 x 3/4 x 1 1/4 in. John Michael Kohler Arts Center Collection, Gift of Mary Nohl. **Page 91, bottom** Untitled (pendant), ca. 1949-75; silver; 1 1/2 x 3 3/4 x 1/8 in. John Michael Kohler Arts Center Collection, Gift of Mary Nohl. **Page 92** Untitled, n.d.; oil on board; 36 x 23 7/8 in. John Michael Kohler Arts Center Collection, Gift of Mary Nohl. **Page 93** Untitled, n.d.; oil on board, 36 x 24 in. Courtesy of Barbara Manger. **Page 94** Untitled, n.d.; oil on board; 15 x 12 in. John Michael Kohler Arts Center Collection. **Page 95** Untitled, n.d.; oil on board; 23 7/8 x 36 in. John Michael Kohler Arts Center Collection, Gift of Mary Nohl. **Page 96** Mary Nohl Lake Cottage Environment (interior site detail, jute sculpture on chair, Fox Point, Wisconsin), John Michael Kohler Arts Center Collection. Photo: 2007, Janine Smith. **Page 97, top** Mary Nohl Lake Cottage Environment (interior site detail, entry hall, Fox Point, Wisconsin), John Michael Kohler Arts Center Collection. Photo: 2004, Scott Dietrich. **Page 97, bottom** Mary Nohl Lake Cottage Environment (interior site detail, Mary's phone, Fox Point, Wisconsin), John Michael Kohler Arts Center Collection. Photo: 2007, Janine Smith. **Page 98** Mary Nohl Lake Cottage Environment (interior site detail, living room, Fox Point, Wisconsin), John Michael Kohler Arts Center Collection. Photo: 2004, Scott Dietrich. **Page 99** Mary Nohl Lake Cottage Environment (site detail, Fox Point, Wisconsin), John Michael Kohler

Arts Center Collection. Photo: 2008, Janine Smith. **Page 100** Mary Nohl Lake Cottage Environment (site detail, fish sculpture, Fox Point, Wisconsin), John Michael Kohler Arts Center Collection. Photo: 2007, Janine Smith. **Page 101, left** Mary Nohl Lake Cottage Environment (site detail, man with fish, Fox Point, Wisconsin), John Michael Kohler Arts Center Collection. Photo: 2007, Janine Smith. **Page 101, right** Mary Nohl Lake Cottage Environment (stone head, Fox Point, Wisconsin), John Michael Kohler Arts Center Collection. Photo: 2008, Janine Smith. **Page 102** Mary Nohl Lake Cottage Environment (site detail, four seated figures, Fox Point, Wisconsin), John Michael Kohler Arts Center Collection. Photo: 2007, Janine Smith. **Page 103, left** Mary Nohl Lake Cottage Environment (site detail, red stick man on house, Fox Point, Wisconsin), John Michael Kohler Arts Center Collection. Photo: 2007, Janine Smith. **Page 103, right** Mary Nohl Lake Cottage Environment (site detail, seated couple, Fox Point, Wisconsin), John Michael Kohler Arts Center Collection. Photo: 2007, Janine Smith. **Page 104** Mary Nohl Lake Cottage Environment (site detail, Fox Point, Wisconsin), John Michael Kohler Arts Center Collection. Photo: 2008, Eric Oxendorf.

Index

This index points you to the pages where you can read about persons, places, and ideas. If you do not find the word you are looking for, try to think of another word that means about the same thing.

When you see a page number in **bold** it means there is a picture on that page.